Strategy and Plans

Leadership Challenges for Servant Leaders

John J. Sullivan

Copyright © 2012 John J. Sullivan
All rights reserved.
ISBN: 13: 978-1470039509
ISBN-10: 1470039508

Other books by John J. Sullivan

Servant First! Leadership for the New Millennium, Xulon Press, 2004

Seven Virtues, The Adventures of John Mouse, Xulon Press, 2010

Books in the series, Leadership Challenges for Servant Leaders:

My Betrayer is at Hand, CreateSpace, 2012

Details, Details, Details, CreateSpace, 2012

Truth Telling, CreateSpace, 2012

Severing the Ties That Bind, CreateSpace, 2012

Good News -- Bad News, CreateSpace, 2012

Eliminate Goal-Setting?, CreateSpace, 2012

Strategy and Plans, CreateSpace, 2012

Dedicated to leaders who
have a vision for a better
tomorrow

"For I know the plans that I have for you, declares the LORD, plans for welfare and not for calamity to give you a future and a hope."
-- Jeremiah 29.11

"Where there is no vision,
the people are unrestrained..."
-- Proverbs 29:11

Preface

This is the seventh monograph in a series which addresses the most common leadership challenges in organizations today. Although the challenges are similar across organizations, the leadership styles which confront them are varied.

Leadership is leadership, whether one leads a small fellowship group or a large corporation, a squad or a corps, a team or an institution. What changes are the language (terms, acronyms) and the rules of engagement (how you interact with followers).

Interestingly, the more senior one becomes the more important are interpersonal relationships. This is counterintuitive at first glance but consider that as one leads larger and more complex organizations one becomes less and less an expert in what the organization does. The further one gets from "the product" the less one knows the product. Senior leaders become increasingly dependent upon followers who have the product expertise they lack; therefore the ability to build and maintain strong interpersonal relationships with core individuals within organizations is key to upper mobility and senior leader success.

This series is aimed at servant leaders or what Jim Collins calls Level 5 leaders[1]. This leadership model is best exemplified by the leadership style of Jesus of Nazareth who said He came to serve and not to be

---

[1] Collins, Jim, *Good to Great: Why Some Companies Make the Leap . . . and Others Don't*, HarperCollins, 2001

served.   Leaders in industry, government, not-for-profit organizations and churches are discovering that the servant leader model is highly effective across organizational types.

This upside-down leadership style puts the needs of followers above those of the leader; promotes teamwork, individual dignity and worth; and results in a synergy of purpose unachievable with the old leadership models.   Its application in today's organizations creates an environment in which people freely choose to create, innovate, and strive for excellence.

Enjoy this monograph on strategic assessment and planning and look for more books in this series *Leadership Challenges for Servant Leaders*.

Contents

John J. Sullivan

Introduction

Every leader of every organization should periodically do a strategic assessment; and every leader of every organization should have a strategic plan that they intend to implement or are implementing. This is equally true for servant leaders. For a new organization these may be a part of the formal business plan. For existing organizations, they form the core of long-range strategic planning and are the blueprint or template for operational planning.

I will describe a Strategic Assessment and Plan that may be utilized by any type of organization, be it a for-profit business or a not-for-profit organization. If yours is a new organization, you may find that the assessment phases 1 and 2 are most helpful. If yours is an existing organization, the assessment phases will help you identify your current state while the planning phases (3 and 4) will point you in the direction you will want to go.

The Strategic Assessment and Plan has four phases and ten steps

The Strategic Assessment and Plan has four phases and ten steps. Each of the steps has a set of questions that, taken as a whole, form the plan. The answers to the questions posed in the phases and

1

steps provide the guidance and direction needed for sustained health and future growth. The phases are:

Phase 1: Where are we?
Phase 2: Where do we want to go?
Phase 3: How are we going to get there?
Phase 4: Are we getting there?

1

Where Are We?

In this assessment phase we will determine our mission, the leader's responsibilities, and analyze the environment in which our organization exists or functions. **The first step is to determine our mission**. What is our purpose, our reason for being? Mission involves what we do now, here in the present. It may change in the future, and probably will, but at least for now, this is what we do. At this point, don't worry too much about crafting a mission statement (assuming you don't have one). That can come later. For now, focus on identifying what it is you do as an organization. Later on you can refine a succinct, coherent statement of your mission.

Next we ask what *business*

Had the railroad companies recognized that they were in the business of moving people and products over long distances, today they would be vertically integrated with other means of transportation

3

are we in? This requires a wide-angle view of our mission and vision for the future. For example, had the railroad companies in the 19th century recognized that they were in the business of moving people and heavy, bulky products over long distances, today they would be vertically integrated with other means of transportation to include airlines, ships, and trucks. Instead, they saw themselves as providing "rail transportation" for people and things. Others own the airlines, shipping and trucking companies. Their vision for the future was too small! Recently some friends took a trip to Alaska. The trip was booked through a vacation cruise company but involved airline transportation, rail transportation, accommodation at a luxury hotel, as well as several days spent cruising on the ship. All of these were owned by the cruise line, with the exception of the airline transportation. This is an example of a company that understands that they are in the business of providing a memorable vacation through the use of different venues and transportation mediums horizontally and vertically integrated.

Who are our customers? Our "customers" are those individuals or organizations who receive our "products" whatever they may be, past, present, and future. Who are we serving now? Who would we like to serve in the future? Determining our customer's needs will form the critical component of our future plan, i.e., how can we best meet those needs? Do we know our customer's demographics? What about lost customers? Determining why customers do not return

New customers can cost up to ten times the cost of retaining existing customers

to your organization can be difficult and time-consuming but the answers can save you future defections. And since new customers can cost up to ten times the cost of retaining existing customers, it will be money well spent (Heebsh, 2006).

Some organizations resist the concept of identifying "customers." This is especially true in education. Who *is* the customer? Is it the student, the parent, local businesses, the community? By wrestling with that question, you may find that you have several classes of customers. For example, I believe that education *does* have more than one customer. I can argue that students receive the "product" of education from faculty and staff and are therefore the "customers" of a school. At another level, I can argue that the educated student is really the "product" of that institution and the employer of its graduates is the true "customer." We can also argue that parents who fund the school (through taxes or tuition) are the true "customers" and must be satisfied. We can see that some organizations may have multiple "customers" whose needs are important and must be met in order for the organization to be successful.

> Discovering the leadership approach required of your subordinates means you must first determine each person's level of competency and commitment

The second step in Phase 1 is to identify the leader's responsibilities, leadership style and values. Ultimately, the leader is responsible for everything that the organization does or does not do. A couple of years ago a U.S. Navy nuclear submarine ran aground on an uncharted sandbar while running submerged. The captain was not at the helm yet he was held accountable and was relieved of his command when the boat returned to port. The U.S. Navy understands that the captain is ultimately responsible for the safe conduct of his vessel even when he is not physically overseeing its course; just so every organization. Does that mean that the leader should retain all responsibility unto himself and delegate nothing? Absolutely not, in fact the leader should seek to delegate all responsibilities except those few that he and he alone must do. This frees him up to concentrate on his most important tasks and creates future leaders who learn as they are delegated responsibility. Therefore, in this step we seek to identify those things that only the leader can do. The number of tasks in every organization will be small because most things can be delegated. Examples of leader-only functions might include: evaluating senior staff, administering the Sacraments, or working with senior community leaders.

Next, we examine leadership style. Don't misunderstand me, as I am not advocating abandonment of the servant-leader approach--by no means! Recent stories in the business press have highlighted companies that are apparently pulling out of a downward spiral after replacing their celebrity CEOs. Under new, low-key, people-focused leaders who seek out the counsel of their subordinates, several major corporations are effecting a turnaround. As Jim Collins discovered in researching for his book, *Good to Great*, all of the eleven "great" CEOs were self-effacing, quiet and reserved yet driven for *organizational* success (Collins, 2001). He called them Level 5 leaders; I call them servant leaders. I believe this approach to leadership, as exemplified by Jesus of Nazareth, is the best model for leading people.[2] He taught that people must be led one person at a time.

Discovering the leadership approach required of your subordinates means you must first determine each person's level of **competency** and **commitment**. Competency refers to the level of expertise and efficiency for the task assigned. Someone who has multiple tasks may have multiple levels of competency; i.e., they may be very good at one task but less so at another. Evaluation of competency is *task-specific*. The degree of leader involvement is dependent upon the *task* and not the individual. In other words, you may need to be more involved in coaching and guiding someone who has low competency with a specific task but have little direct involvement with other tasks where their competency level is high.

Organizational commitment is *global* in nature. That is, ones level of commitment to the success of the organization is not dependent upon a specific task. The leader's challenge with this type of person is to move them from an "enrolled" status to one of commitment. A person who is merely enrolled is one who does what is required, nothing more, nothing less. She has no long-term interest in the organization and displays little or no loyalty. On the

---

[2] For a complete discussion of Jesus as leader see the author's book, *Servant First! Leadership for the New Millennium*, Xulon Press, 2004.

other hand, a person who is truly committed to an organization takes the initiative to do what needs to be done for the organization to be successful. She does not wait to be told her job, she seeks out ways to improve, refine, and build quality and efficiency.

Leaders should examine their staff and seek to discover each person's level of competency and commitment and then decide the level of leader involvement and delegated responsibility appropriate to each. This does not mean foregoing an overall servant-leader approach. It does mean that you will be more involved on a daily basis with some employees and less with others.

The final substep involves a comparison of organizational values and the leader's personal values. Are the two in agreement? If not, then the leader must take some action to either change the culture of the organization or his personal values. In an entrepreneurial start-up, organizational values generally reflect the leader's values. In an existing organization, the inherited values of an organization may have changed over its lifespan and are no longer healthy to growth. This can frequently happen as an organization becomes larger and begins to take on the negative qualities of a bureaucracy (not that *all* bureaucratic characteristics are negative). For example, with the introduction of competition in the telecommunication industry, telephone companies who formerly operated a monopoly are now faced with a new model for customer service. Those companies who will consistently provide superior customer service at a fair price will be successful. Others who do not treat customers as assets will not survive.

The third and final step in Phase 1 is to analyze the environments in which an organization exists, internally and externally. What are our distinctive competencies and our competitive advantage? This is often referred to as SWOT analysis: strengths and weaknesses (internally), and opportunities and threats (externally). What are our own organizational strengths? What are our distinctive competencies and our competitive advantage, i.e., what sets us apart from others that have the same or similar mission? For a business, this means asking why should a customer do business with us over one of our competitors? For a non-profit, such as a church, it means asking why should a family attend our church rather than another church closer to home? An organization that cannot identify its competitive advantage is doomed to failure. So if you don't know what your competitive advantage is, you might as well get out of business now and save yourself the headaches of certain failure in the future. But it may also include: location, availability and education of the workforce, cost control, quality level, worker satisfaction, use of technology and the like. What are our weaknesses? These may include many of the same categories listed under strengths. We must be brutally honest here and seek to build on our strengths and mitigate our weaknesses.

As we look to the external environment, we identify our competitors and not only those who offer a similar product but also those who have a product that may be substituted for ours. For example, a company operating a golf driving range and batting cages needs to look beyond other driving ranges/batting cages and consider companies offering recreation services as potential competitors. What are the strengths and weaknesses of our competitors? Consider factors such as: location, level of technology, prices, reputation, longevity, community involvement, and customer service. What are the barriers to entry to our business/industry? What are the opportunities and threats in the external environment? Is the local government a threat or an opportunity? Companies operating internationally will consider this as one of the major environmental factors. Consider other factors such as: number of competitors, regulations, environmental constraints, natural resources, transportation infrastructure and the state of the economy.

Once we have done a thorough assessment of our current condition, we turn to the question of what do we want to become?

2

Where Do We Want To Go?

Here we look to the future by working through the next four steps to develop our vision and organizational values; identify key processes and systems; determine gaps in performance; and finally, establish objectives and goals.

You will recall that in Phase 1 we developed our mission, i.e., our purpose, our reason for being. Mission is what we do NOW; it is oriented to the present. Vision is what we hope to do in the future. It is a unifying picture of where the organization is going and enables everyone to focus on the same distant point on the horizon. Our mission may change as we move toward our vision

The proof that we have the vision is that we are reaching out for more than we have grasped.
--Oswald Chambers

over time but our vision should remain. Mission and vision form two elements of the organization's Guiding Principles. The third element is values, which will be discussed below (Sullivan, 2004).

Step 4 is development of the organizational vision and values. That vision should be a *shared vision*. It will not be effective as a guiding principle if it is only the leader's vision. The leader has an important role to play in visioning but his role cannot be as the sole author and enforcer of the vision. A vision statement crafted by a leader or even an executive group without input and critique from the people within the organization will not become a shared vision. Sorry, it just won't happen. So how do we achieve a shared vision?

Servant leaders know that people are more committed to decisions when they have been involved in the decision process. Even if an individual's opinions and ideas are not accepted along the path to a final decision, the fact that you listened to them and considered their input is vital to their commitment to implementation. Therefore it is important that as many people as possible in the organization have an opportunity to provide input on the organizational vision statement. Practically, how do you do that?

Here is where the leader comes in because without the leader's active involvement there will be no vision. (See Proverbs 29:18) The leader must *initiate* the discussion of a vision of a future state, an organization that we hope to become. She may even have a small group of people draft a vision statement after talking to as many people in the organization as possible about what they see in the future for our organization. Once this is done, I like Stephen Covey's recommendation to send the statement out with an invitation to critique it that reads something like this: *"Here is the draft vision statement. We don't much like it either so we'd like to hear from you!"* (Covey, 1989). That gives license to tear it apart. If you don't do that then it becomes the "boss' vision statement" and your people will be fearful to openly criticize it. Your only input will be laudatory comments that do nothing to create commitment to the vision.

The third element in our organizational Guiding Principles is values, i.e., how will we treat each other and our "customers" (those we serve) on our way toward our vision? In the first phase, we discussed the leader's values and how they must examine their own set of values and how they relate to the organization. In this step, we are determining what those organizational values currently are, or if this is a new organization, what we want them to be. Organizational values that form and shape the organizational culture are often unspoken but are simply "the way we do things around here." A new leader coming in to an existing organization may be surprised to learn the dominant values practiced in the organization. What is down on paper and the "way things really work" may be two entirely different things. Ask lots of questions and values will emerge. It may take setting up a series of scenarios: if this happens, how do we deal with it? For example: What do we tell a customer when a shipment will be late especially if he represents a large percentage of our total sales?

How are we going to treat each other *within* the organization? What level of trust are we comfortable with? For example, an organization that trusts and

13

respects its employees will not hesitate to share its financial details. The company is saying, in effect: *we trust you and respect your judgment and opinions such that we are willing to disclose our most intimate financial details with you since this is your company too!* However, you must live out those values for them to become truly a part of the culture. Southwest Airlines is famous for its customer service. They live out their value of putting customers' needs first. However, if the day arrives where an employee is disciplined for taking too much time with a customer that value dies. The old value is replaced with "speed = profit" and the needs of customers move to the back of the line. So be careful what you say you value because your people will be watching to see if you really mean it.

Step 5 is to identify your key processes and systems. What are the few key systems and processes that differentiate us from our competitors and give us competitive advantage? Most organizations do lots of things but there are a few, select systems and processes that set the organization apart from others that are critical. We must do these well or we will not survive as an organization. The great football coach Vince Lombardi was very successful, in part, because he focused on the essentials: tackling and blocking. What is essential to the success of your organization? What are those systems and processes that are most important to its survival? For example, a liberal arts college must provide good, sound classroom instruction in order to survive. They do lots of other things but classroom instruction is critical to the future of the organization. Likewise, the manufacturing processes of an automobile maker are critical to its success. If they

14

don't build a quality automobile, all the glib marketing in the world won't save it from ruin. For a church, the Sunday worship service is a critical system or series of processes involving facilities, music, prayers, scripture reading, a message preached, and the coordination of a host of people. A beautiful campus or an award-winning day care facility will not keep the doors of that church open; focusing on the critical systems will.

Step 6 is to determine the gaps in performance in our key systems and processes. We do this because we know that these systems and processes are essential to our survival and we must do them well. The Pareto Principle states that 80% of consequences stem from 20% of the causes (Reh, 2006). Therefore we should focus on those few essential systems and processes, as they will impact most of the other systems within the organization. First, we must gather data on our current level of performance in our key systems and processes. The metrics we choose are also critical since we must find what truly measures our *effectiveness* and that can take some time and trial. For example, the number of hours an employee spends in professional growth seminars is *not* a good metric for their level of training. What the person is able to *do* with the new knowledge is what you want to measure. Finding a metric that does that is the challenge.

Once we feel that we have a good understanding of the steady state performance of our key systems, then we compare that condition with our desired future state. How do we determine what the standard should be? One way is to look to those organizations in whatever industry that consistently produce world-class results in a given area or system. If you were to stop by the L.L. Bean headquarters in Freeport, Maine, today you would see people from all over the world who are not there to purchase items from the L.L. Bean retail store—although they may indulge a bit. They are there to learn how L.L. Bean is able to produce, market, and ship their many products all over the world with great efficiency, accuracy and timeliness. L.L. Bean *is* the world standard and thankfully they are willing to share their expertise with others.

As we compare our key processes and systems against such standards, are there gaps in performance? In most cases, there will be. Now our task is to develop objectives and goals to close those gaps.

Step 7, the final step in Phase 2, is where we establish strategic and operational objectives that once obtained, will close the gaps in performance in our key systems and processes. The terms "objectives" and "goals" are sometimes interchanged but I prefer to use the term objective to mean an over-arching or super-goal and goals as a series of measurable targets leading up to an objective. *Strategic* objectives are those longer-term objectives that will take 3-5 years to complete. That is the time frame generally accepted as long-term, at least in the West. Eastern cultures tend to think in much long terms as witnessed by Konosuke

John J. Sullivan

Matsushita, founder and CEO of Matsushita Electric, the global Japanese electronics firm, who some years ago asked his senior executives to think 250 years out (Clawson, 2006). Jesus' challenge to "... go make disciples of all the nations, baptizing them in the name of the Father and the Son and the Holy Spirit," (Matthew 29:19) is a strategic objective many centuries out!

Operational objectives are to be completed within a year. An example of a strategic objective for a manufacturing company might be to **develop new product lines for Eastern Europe**. An operational objective supporting this could be to **develop and market one new product for Eastern Europe.** A strategic objective for an urban church could be to **establish a youth drop-in center for teens** or **develop and implement parenting skills training for single parents**.

Goals then are established under each objective that leads to completion of at least one element of that objective. These goals must be SMART: specific, measurable, achievable, results-oriented, and time-determined. For example:

Strategic Objective: **Develop new product lines for Eastern Europe**
Goal: **Within 90 days, determine customer needs for our products and available suppliers within Eastern Germany**

Specific: determine needs and suppliers within Eastern Germany
Measurable: listing of expressed product needs and outlets for supply
Achievable: we believe this can be done in the time

allotted
Results-oriented: specific results have been identified
Time-determined: complete within three months

Strategic Objective: Establish a youth drop-in center for teens
Goal: By January 1, create a prioritized listing of available suitable existing buildings listed under $500,000 within 3 miles of church

Specific: determine inventory of available, suitable building near our facility
Measurable: physical count of buildings meeting our criteria
Achievable: we believe this can be done in the time allotted
Results-oriented: specific results have been identified
Time-determined: a deadline has been established

Each objective may have several goals. The more complex the objective the more goals we can expect. Objectives must support the mission and vision of the organization. Likewise, goals will support one or more objectives. Objectives that are not directly tied to furthering the organization's mission and vision should not be considered.

3

How Are We Going To Get There?

This phase, which has a single step, requires the development of an implementation plan and systems for monitoring performance.

Step 8 involves development of an implementation plan for the objectives and goals determined in Phase 2. Remember that each objective and its associated goal(s) are carefully selected to close a measurable gap between our current level of performance in key systems and processes and the desired future state. For each goal, we must determine:

- Who will be assigned responsibility for completion of the goal?
- What steps are to be accomplished?
- What resources will be made available?
- How should the work be accomplished?
- When do we want the goal completed?

Who will be held responsible for accomplishing the goal? This involves *delegation* of responsibility from a leader to a subordinate. This must be done since a task cannot simply be assigned to a group of people with the expectation that they will accept the responsibility and accomplish the task. Someone must be held directly responsible.

Successful delegation involves three elements: *responsibility*, *authority* and *accountability*. When a leader assigns *responsibility* for a task to a subordinate, he is, in effect, transferring *his* responsibility to that person. As discussed in Phase 1, the leader is responsible for everything the organization does or does not do. But he can and must delegate direct responsibility for tasks to subordinates. In order for the person to effectively accomplish the task assigned, he must also receive the *authority* to call upon resources needed to accomplish the goal. Those resources may include people, material, technology, funds, equipment, time, or whatever is needed to get the job done. Finally, the person assigned will be held accountable for accomplishment of the task. Failure to perform a delegated task successfully is usually attributable to the leader's failure at delegating one of the essential elements. Often, that element is authority.

> Failure to perform a delegated task successfully is usually attributable to the leader's failure at delegating one of the essential elements

The Gospels record Jesus delegating responsibility to His disciples as He prepared them to assume leadership: "... Jesus called together his twelve apostles and gave them *power* and *authority* to cast out demons and to heal all diseases. Then he sent

20

them out to tell everyone about the coming of the Kingdom of God and to heal the sick" (*emphasis* added. Luke 9:1,2). When He had finished delegating these responsibilities, Jesus "… went off teaching and preaching in towns throughout the country" (Matthew 11:1). Not long after delegating authority to heal and exorcise, we see evidence that Jesus delegated other leadership responsibilities to his disciples in the feeding of the five thousand. Confronted with their plea to "send the crowds away to the nearby villages and farms, so they can find food and lodging for the night," (Matthew 9:12), Jesus turns to the disciples and commands, "*You* feed them," (*emphasis* added. Matthew 9:13). Jesus has made clear to these His future leaders that He has delegated not only the *responsibility* to care for the people but also the *authority* to call upon resources to successfully complete each task.

The steps to be accomplished are a series of events that must be completed in order for the goal to be realized. At this level they should be generalized while leaving the details to the person assigned and their team to determine. The same principle applies to the question of how should the work be accomplished. Leave the details to the leader and their team to determine how best to accomplish the steps.

The resources needed to accomplish the task must be authorized or assigned by the senior leader whenever they exceed the normal level of authority of the delegated leader. This is best done in writing and formal notice given to other senior leaders in the organization of the delegated leader's authority and the duration of the task. This is especially important when people from another part of the organization may be required to assist in task accomplishment.

21

Strategy and Plans

Assigning a date/time for goal accomplishment makes very clear to all when the job must be completed. If follow on tasks will depend upon completion of the task assigned, the person assigned and their team should also know this.

One way to display goals is with a grid, as depicted in Table 1, below.

Table 1

GOAL	WHO?	STEPS	RESOURCES	HOW?	WHEN?
Determine customer needs in E. Germany	Roger Smith's team in marketing	1. Survey potential customers 2. Determine substitutes 3. Identify brand loyalty	1. Smith's team of 4 2. Direct mailing up to 20,000 homes 3. Funds necessary for analytic reporting by contractor	1. By random survey 2. Suppliers within E. Germany 3. Buyers for major retail chains	Final report by 15 July
Determine suitable space for youth center	Jim Brown, Youth Minister	1. Determine our youth population over next 15 years 2. Determine square footage and facilities needed 3. Identify available structures w/i 3 mile radius	1. Brown + Facility Director 2. Church Realty Division 3. Church sedan	1. Review projected demographic growth in youth population 2. Survey our youth & other churches with youth centers for facility needs 3. Major realtors for buildings availability 4. Prioritized list of buildings under $500K	Preliminary report by 1 Dec; final report by 1 Jan

Critical to the success of the implementation plan is the integration of the overall strategic plan with operational plans, and their associated budgets, and personnel evaluation. This insures that operational plans and goals flow from and directly support the strategic plan and that subordinate leaders are evaluated based on the results of goal accomplishment.

Finally we turn to the fourth phase where we will establish a review process for changing our strategic direction and ensuring that our plan stays fresh and relevant over time.

Strategy and Plans

4

Are We Getting There?

These two last steps involve monitoring performance, analyzing feedback, review and evaluation. This is the phase most often overlooked or underappreciated but critical to the success of our strategic plan. is an old but true proverb. Therefore, as discussed in Step 6, our choice of metrics is vitally important to goal achievement. Do we measure *effectiveness*, i.e., doing the right things, or *efficiency*, i.e., doing things right?

What gets measured gets done

Step 9, therefore, is where we determine how we will measure objective/goal accomplishment and identify other means for progress feedback. This step is often overlooked because it is difficult and frequently frustrating to determine the measures that will tell you what you need to know. The fast and easy choices often don't measure our true success or failure. Finding the right metrics can be a process of trial and error. That's why it is necessary to frequently review and evaluate the data and its associated metric. For example, does counting the number of conferences or workshops attended tell us whether or not a leader understands and can apply

25

servant leadership to his everyday responsibilities? How do we measure the *results* of his education?

Normally, leaders will want to use more than one metric to gain a true perspective on goal accomplishment. Selecting a quantitative *and* a qualitative metric may provide more realistic feedback than simply relying on a quantitative measurement alone. For example, measuring customer satisfaction with a product by tracking the number of complaints received for that product may only tell us part of the story. Talking with customers may reveal that problems with the product have caused customer defections to competing products. The customers are not complaining because they are no longer your customers!

Jesus was debating with some teachers of religious law when one of the men spoke up to say that his son was mute and possessed by an evil spirit, which caused him to have violent seizures. He had taken the boy to Jesus' disciples for healing but they were unable to cast out the evil spirit. When the lad was brought forward, Jesus rebuked the spirit, healed him, and sent father and son happily on their way. Later, His disciples questioned Him as to why they could not cast out the evil spirit. Jesus replied, "This kind can be cast out only by prayer," (Mark 9:14-29). Jesus used feedback from a "customer" to measure the effectiveness of His delegation of responsibility and authority to cast out evil spirits and to heal. He held His disciples responsible for performing the work and when presented with evidence that they were not completely successful, He corrected them and sent them out again.

Step 10 is review and evaluation. Here we determine the process for continued review of our progress on objective/goal accomplishment. How frequently will we review the data? What level of variation (deviation from plan) will cause us to change our implementation plan? What criteria will we use for changing strategic direction? How often will we review our mission and vision? What events would cause us to change? These questions need to be answered with broad participation throughout the organization. I recommend that the senior level of the organization conduct an annual review of its Guiding Principles and its major objectives. Objectives and associated goals should be reviewed at least semiannually at the division level and more frequently (quarterly/monthly) at the next level down.

Dr. Dan Struble, President of Montreat College, insures that the strategic planning process continues throughout the year by holding quarterly MIT (monitoring and implementation team) meetings to evaluate progress, assess changes in the environment and shift priorities, resources and initiatives to reflect the dynamic environment within which the organization operates.

The "ladies and gentlemen" of the Ritz-Carlton chain will be asked to think for themselves

The Ritz-Carlton Hotel chain, long the leader in the luxury hotel sector, recently conducted just such a review. Recognizing the changing demographics in the typical high-end hotel guest, the "name that has defined luxury as a cross between formal elegance and unwavering service" (Sanders 2006, B1) has announced that they are abandoning their 20 rules for dealing with guest requests and adopting instead 12 service values. Rather than adhering to a rigid set of responses for each situation, According to the president and chief executive officer, Simon Cooper, hotel chains in this sector are struggling with how to define luxury in a crowded and evolving market. The typical luxury hotel traveler is no longer necessarily a middle-age male businessman or a wealthy jet-setter but could be a 30-something in a T-shirt and jeans. This new type of guest often doesn't want to be addressed in the old, more formal way. This has caused a reassessment at the very core of what the company stands for. Vivian Deuschl, vice president for public relations, affirmed that the Ritz is not changing their values, rather they are freeing their associates to better meet the needs of guests while maintaining high standards for service (V. Deuschl, personal communication, June 29, 2006). This type of assessment and targeted response to environmental changes are what keep companies like the Ritz-Carlton at the top of their industry.

5

Conclusion

The Strategic Assessment and Plan, as outlined here, provides a way for servant leaders in all types of organizations to broadly involve their people intimately and deeply in the future of the organization. This begins with a collective assessment of the current state of the organization and the environments within which it operates. Once we are confident of our contemporary state, we next determine the future direction for the organization. This may mean holding true to the established course or turning to a new heading based on our shared vision. Then we identify those few, important things that we do that can mean success or failure—our key processes and systems. We closely examine our output in those key areas against world-class standards or what we have determined to be our goals and look for gaps in performance. Where we are able to identify substandard performance, we create objectives and goals to close those gaps. These objectives and goals are then defined by implementation plans laying out the steps required to achieve each objective and goal. Once the plans have been implemented, we must develop feedback mechanisms that will provide us with real-time progress reports. Finally, we must create a review process for reassessing our overall plans and objectives.

By now you have probably come to the conclusion that this is not a quick or simple process. And you are right—it is not! However, it is an effective tool for leaders in all types of organizations to harness the ingenuity and creativity of people and to involve them directly in the future direction of the organization by creating new servant leaders in organizations that add meaning and purpose to their lives and the lives of those they serve.

Appendix A

The Strategic Assessment and Plan
An Outline

Phase 1: Where are we?

1. Determine the mission
   - What is our purpose, reason for existence?
   - What business are we in?
   - Who are our customers?
2. Identify the leader's responsibilities, leadership style & values
   - What are the things only the leader can do? (i.e., what *cannot* be delegated?)
   - What leadership style is required given the circumstances (level of commitment & competency)?
   - How will the leader's own personal values affect the organization?
3. Analyze the external & internal environments
   - What are our own internal strengths & weaknesses?
   - What are our distinctive competencies/competitive advantages?
   - Who are our competitors & what are their strengths & weaknesses?
   - What other external threats & opportunities can we identify?

Phase 2: Where do we want to go?

4. Develop the organizational vision & values
   - What is our vision for the future of our organization?

- What values will we adhere to in dealing with our customers (those we serve), both external & internal?
5. Identify key processes & systems
   - What are the few, key systems & processes that differentiate us from our competitors?
   - What are those systems & processes that are most important to our survival?
6. Determine gaps in performance
   - What is our current level of performance in our key systems & processes?
   - When we compare our current performance with our desired future state, are there gaps in systems or processes?
7. Establish objectives & goals
   - What are the strategic and operational objectives that, once obtained, will close our gaps in performance?
   - What are the necessary goals we will need to achieve in order to accomplish our stated objectives?

Phase 3: How are we going to get there?

8. Develop the implementation plan
For each goal, determine:
   - Who will be assigned responsibility?
   - What steps are to be accomplished?
   - What resources are available?
   - How will the work be accomplished (in general terms)?
   - When do we want the goal completed?

Phase 4: Are we getting there?

9. Monitor performance & feedback analysis

- How will we measure goal accomplishment?
- What other means will we use for feedback on our progress?

10. Review & evaluation
    - What will be the process for continual review of our progress?
    - What criteria will we use for changing strategic direction?

Strategy and Plans

References

Clawson, J., (2006).   Personal and Organizational Charters.
http://faculty.darden.virginia.edu/clawsonj/pdf/ClawCh12v2_072205.pdf (July 8, 2006)

Collins, J.C., (2001).   Good to Great: Why Some Companies Make the Leap...and Others Don't.   New York, NY: HarperCollins Publishers, Inc.

Covey, S.R., (1989).   The 7 Habits of Highly Effective People: Powerful Lessons in Personal Change.   New York, NY: Simon & Schuster, Inc.

Heebsh, A., (2006).   Customers: the new window to profitability.   Teradata Magazine.
http://www.teradata.com/t/page/135376/index.html (June 29, 2006).

Reh, F.J. Pareto's Principle-The 80-20 Rule.   About Management.
http://management.about.com/cs/generalmanagement/a/Pareto081202.htm (June 28, 2006).

Sanders, P., (2006).   Taking' Off the Ritz—a Tad.   Wall Street Journal, June 23, 2006, B1.

Sullivan, J.J., (2004).   Servant First! Leadership for the New Millennium.   Longwood, FL: Xulon Press.

About the Author

John J. Sullivan is the director of ServantLeader Ministries whose mission is to educate, encourage and equip leaders in all walks of life who desire to serve rather than be served.

He has had a wide variety of career experiences. He has served as a Marine Corps fighter pilot, a squadron and air station commander, senior staff officer, consultant, quality examiner, athletics director, professor, and conference commissioner. He is widely acclaimed as an authority on servant leadership as an author, a teacher and a practitioner.

A highly decorated Vietnam veteran, prior to entering academia he served for 28 years in the U.S. Marine Corps as a helicopter gunship pilot, fighter pilot, squadron commander, senior staff officer, base commander, and professor, retiring as a colonel. As a senior staff officer in the Pentagon, he was Program Coordinator for what was then the Department of the Navy's largest development and acquisition program, the F/A-18 Hornet aircraft. While he was the Commanding Officer, Marine Corps Air Station Beaufort, SC, the base was selected in worldwide competition as the best installation in the Marine Corps and received the prestigious Commander-in-Chief's Award for Installation Excellence.

He was the Course Director of Policy Making and Implementation within the National Security Decision Making Department and professor of management at the Naval War College, Newport, RI. He taught in the graduate program primarily in leadership education.

An American Society for Quality Certified Quality Manager, he was a founder of the Rhode Island Area Coalition for Excellence (RACE), helped design its State quality award, and was its first lead examiner.

Following his military career, Sullivan served for nine years as an associate professor of business at Montreat College, Montreat, NC. His teaching focus was in the disciplines of leadership and management.

He is a graduate of the University of Southern California, Webster University and the Naval War College.

Visit http://www.servantleaderministries.org for more information on servant leadership or the author.